If Biden is elected, "They are going to put him in a home and other people are going to be running the country.

- President Donald Trump

LETS PAINT SOME PROOFS...

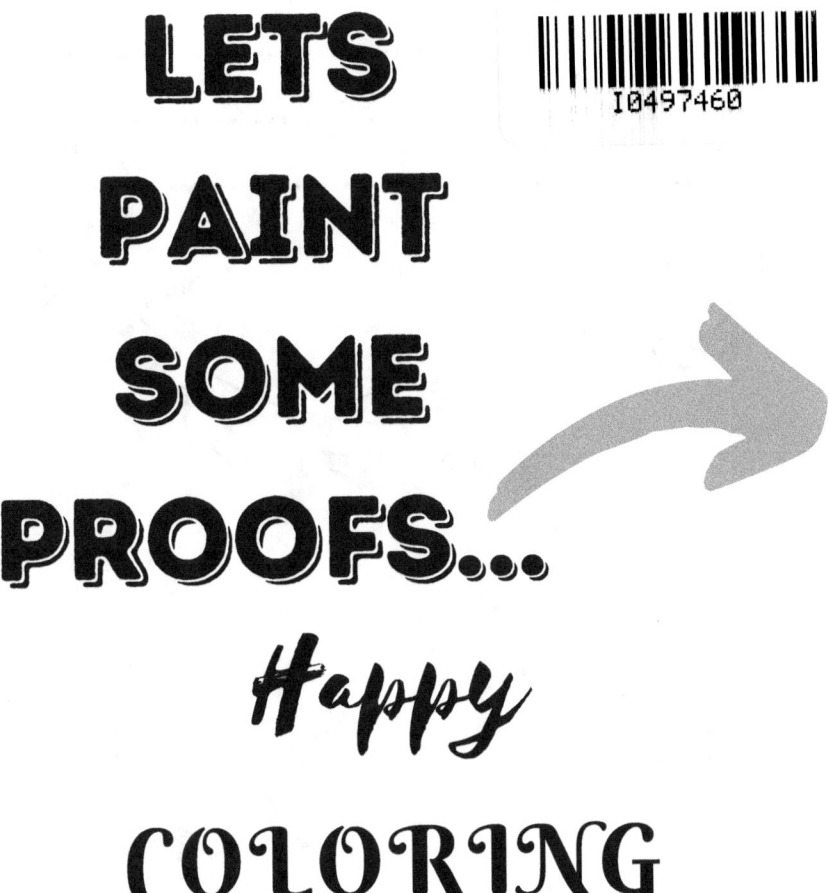

Happy COLORING

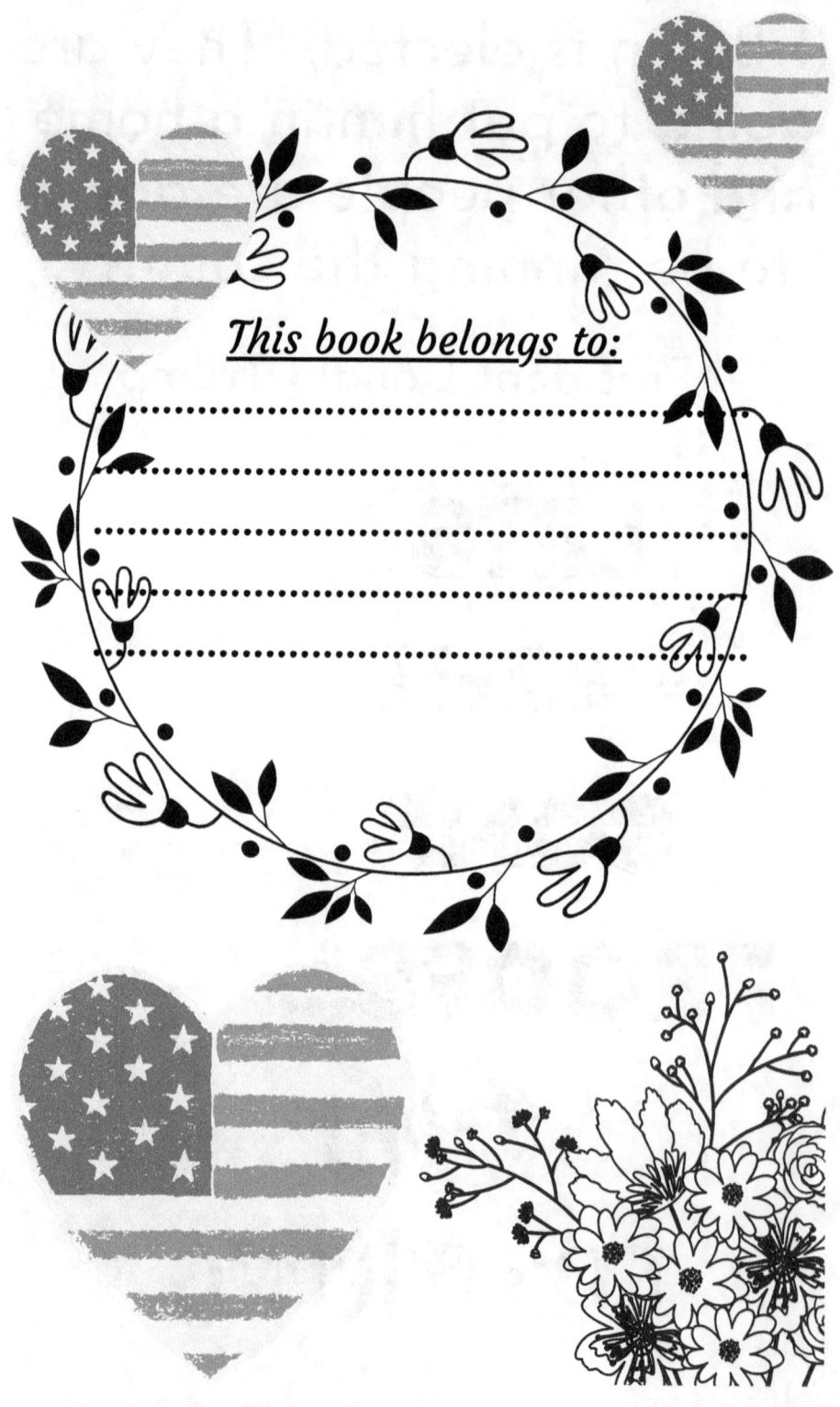

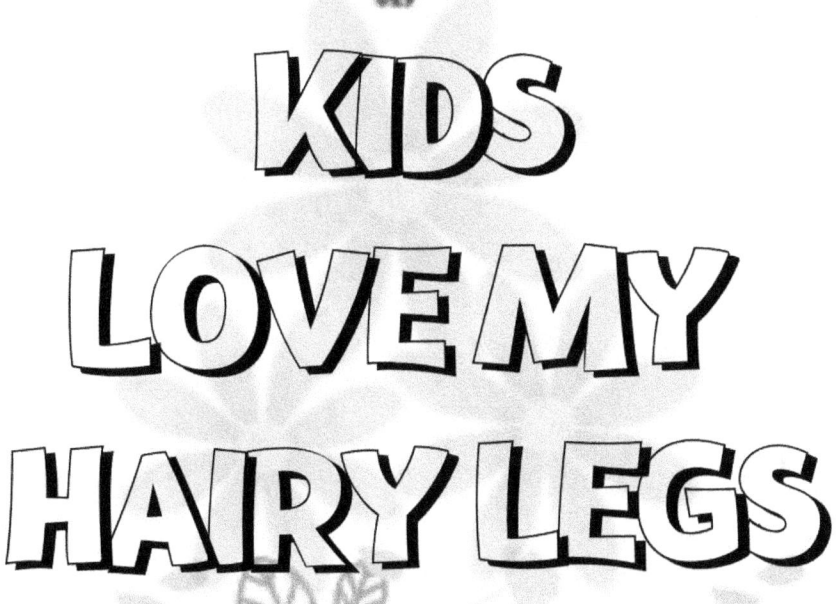

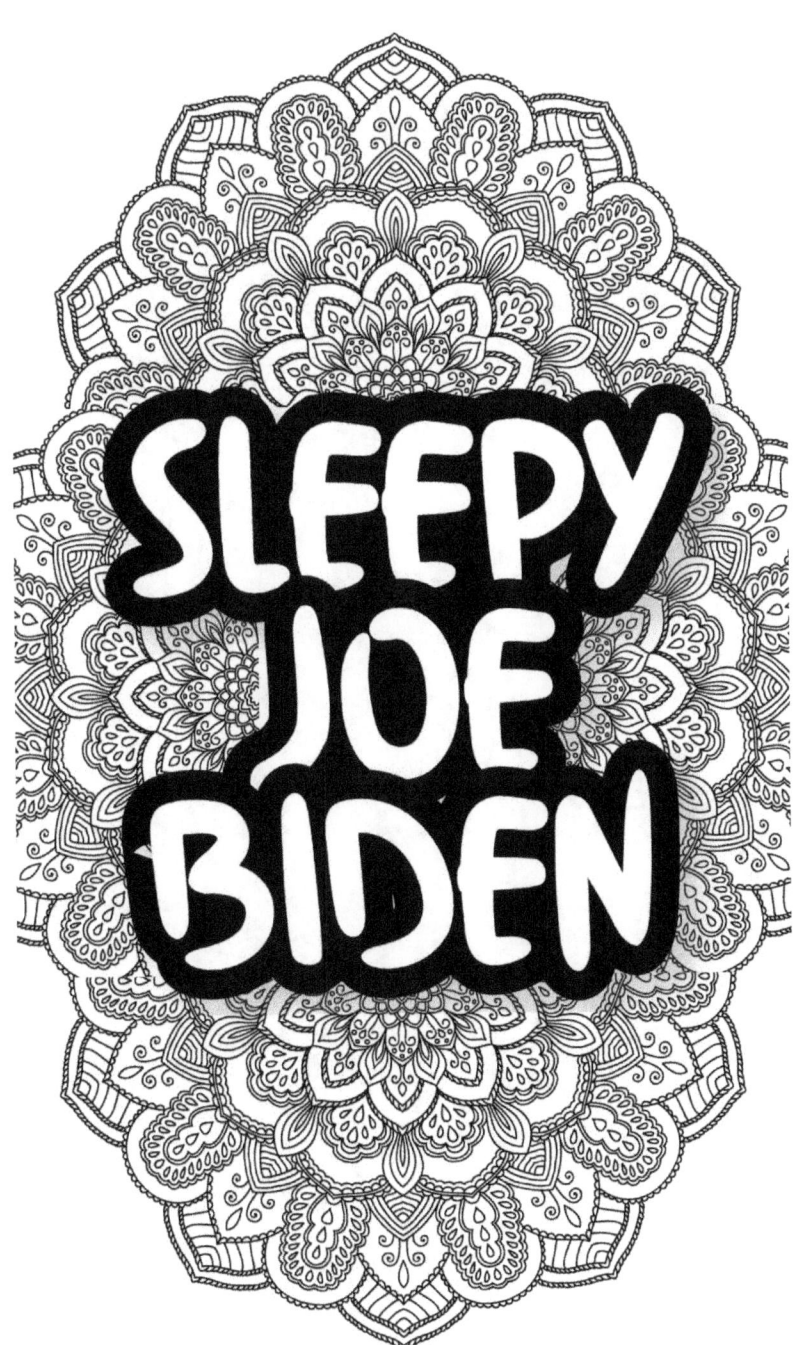

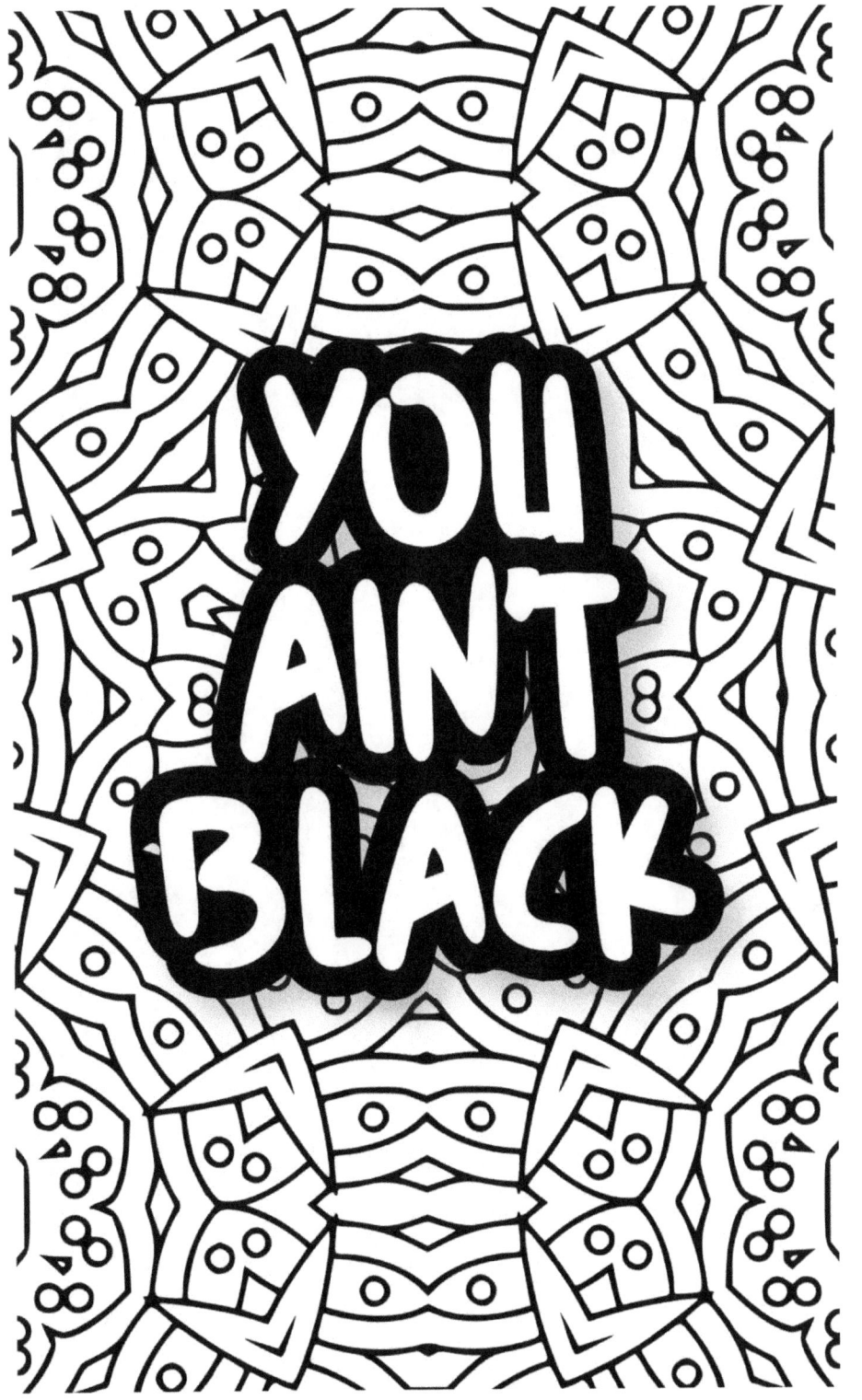

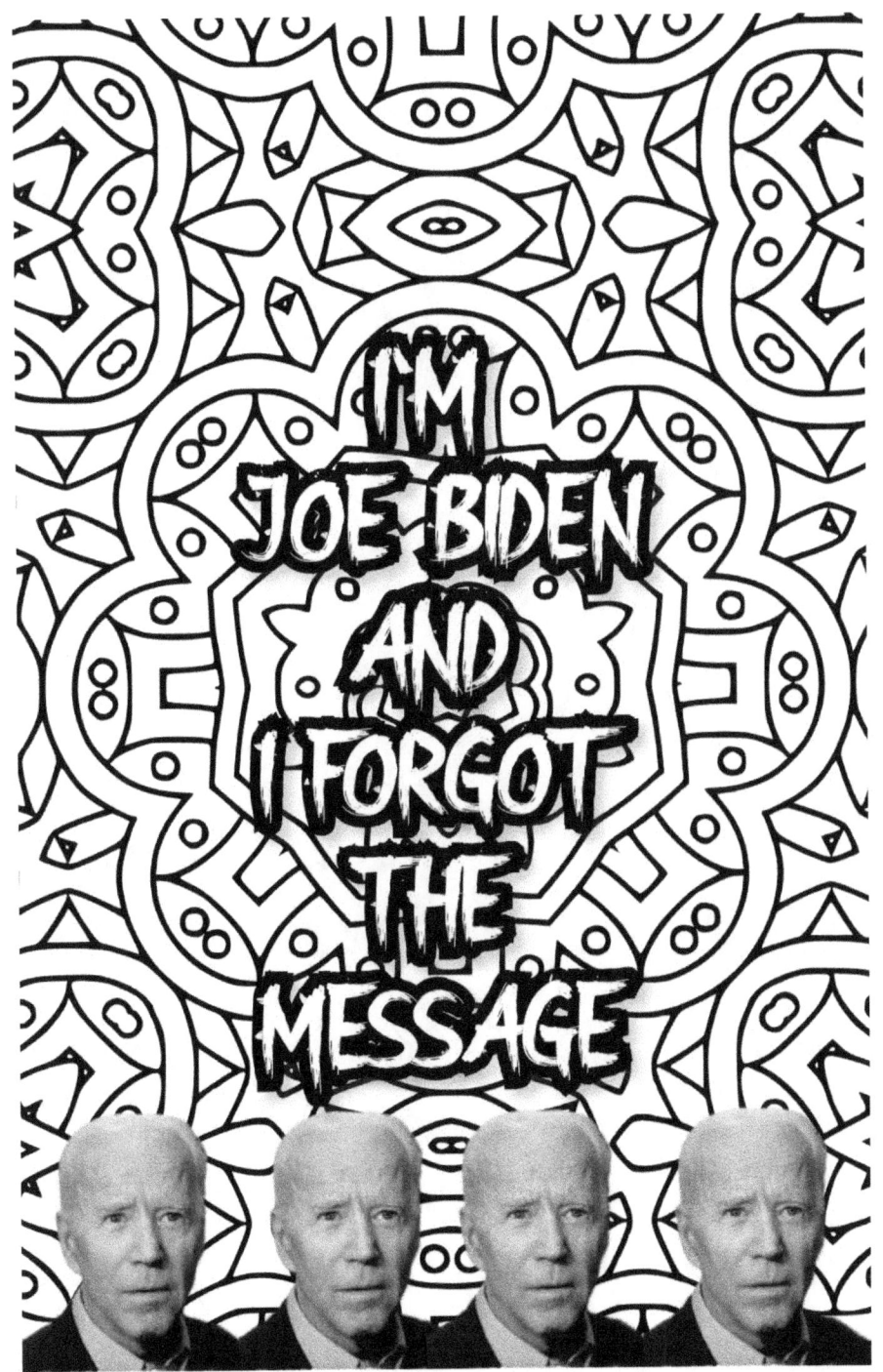

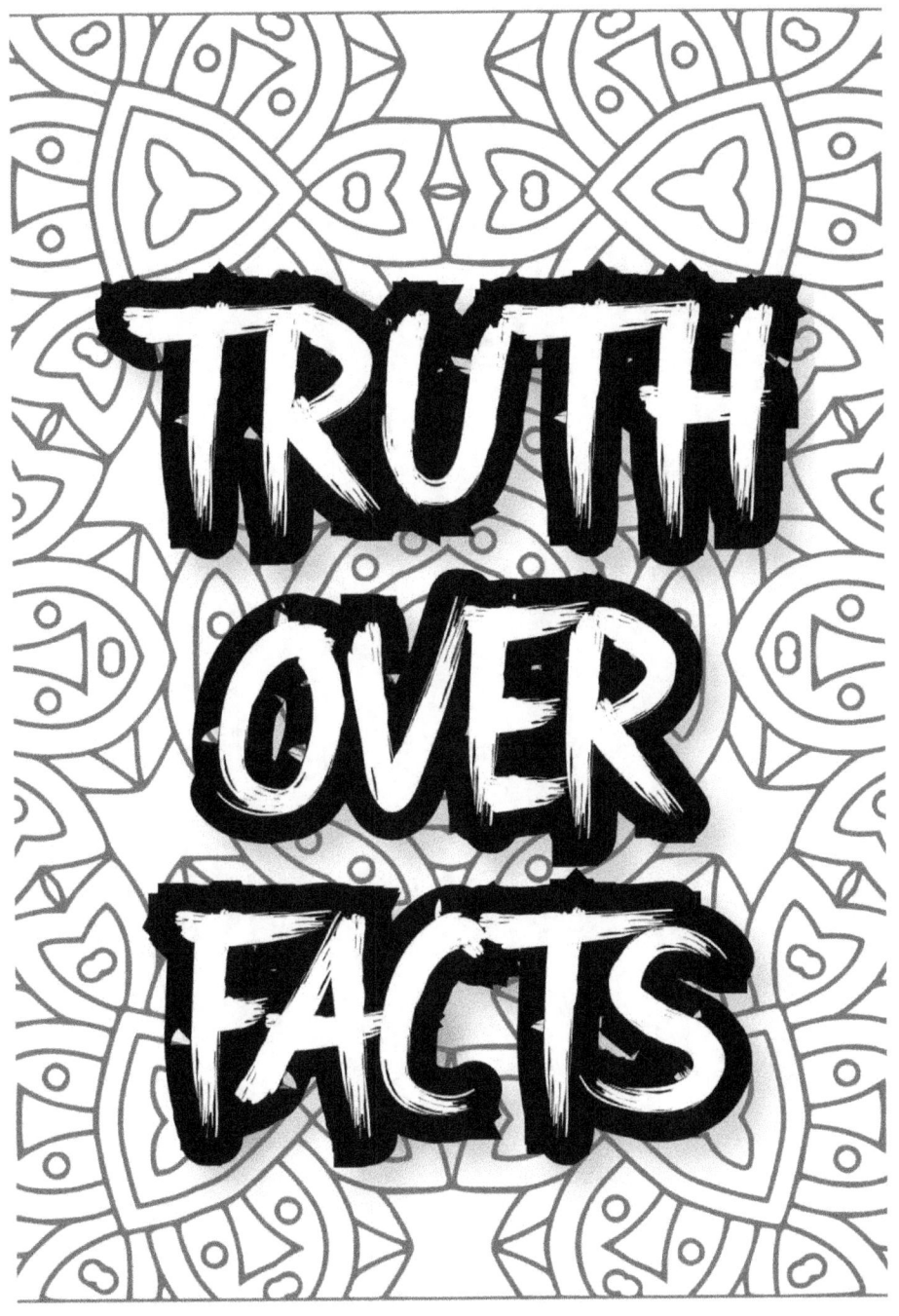

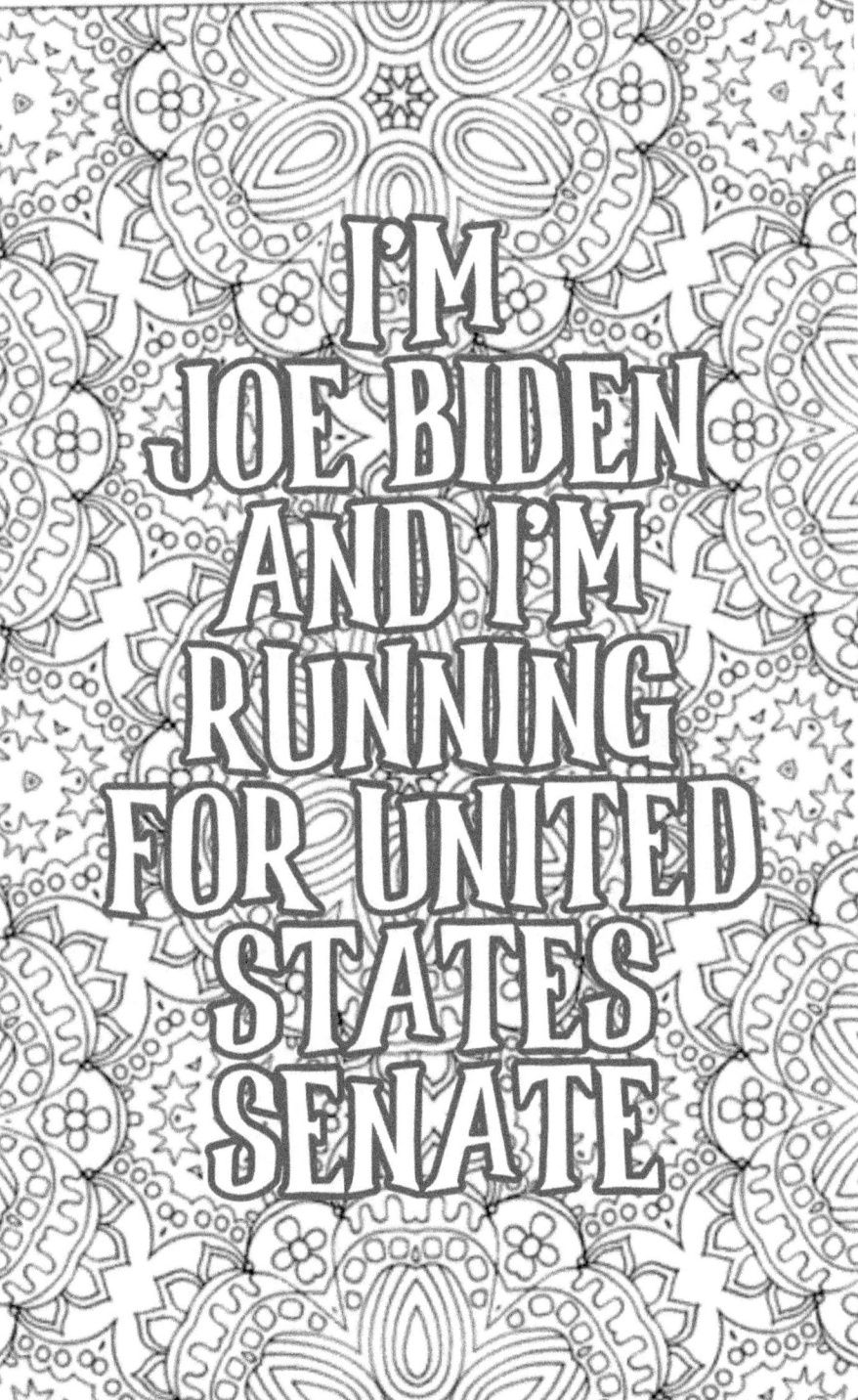

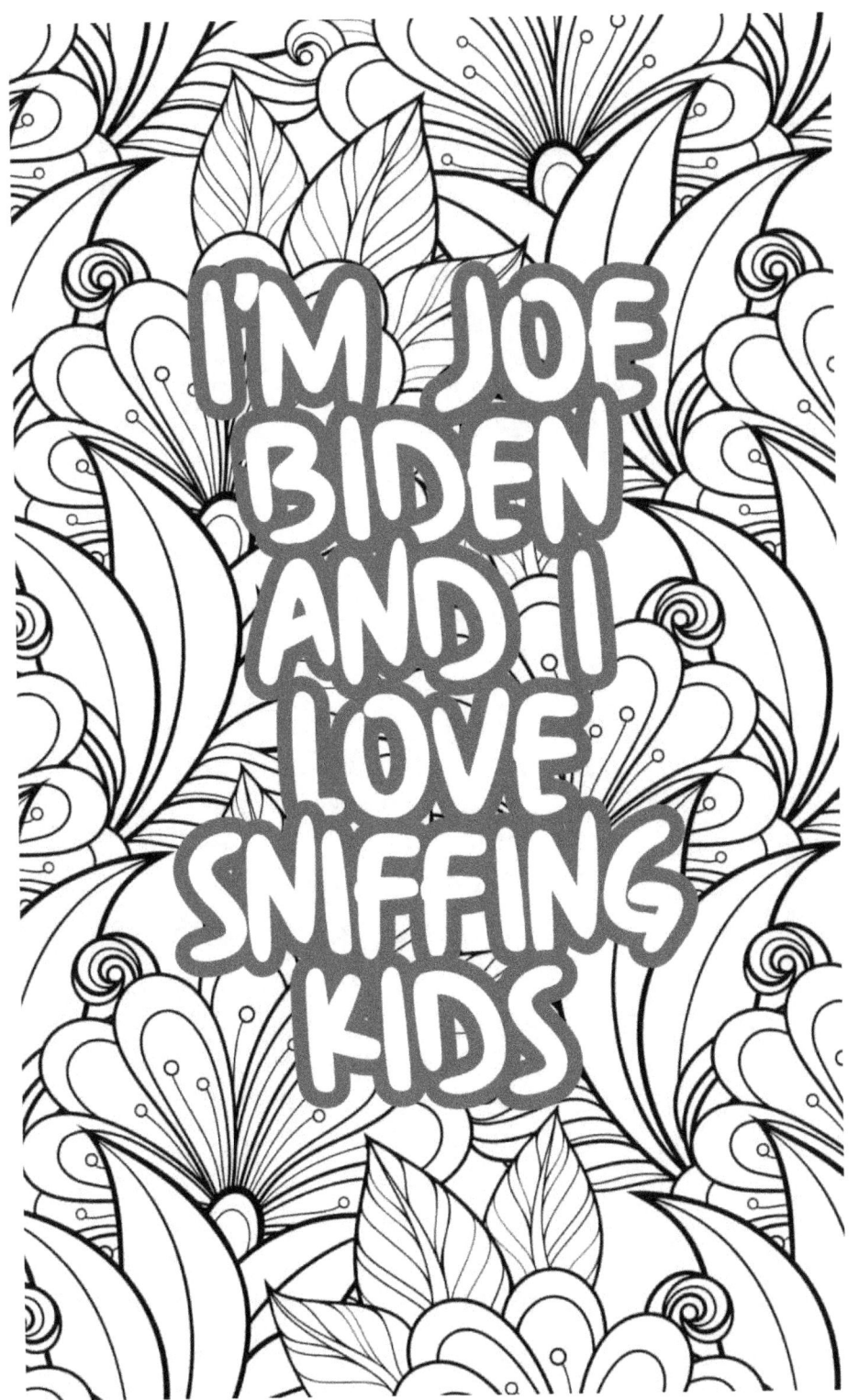

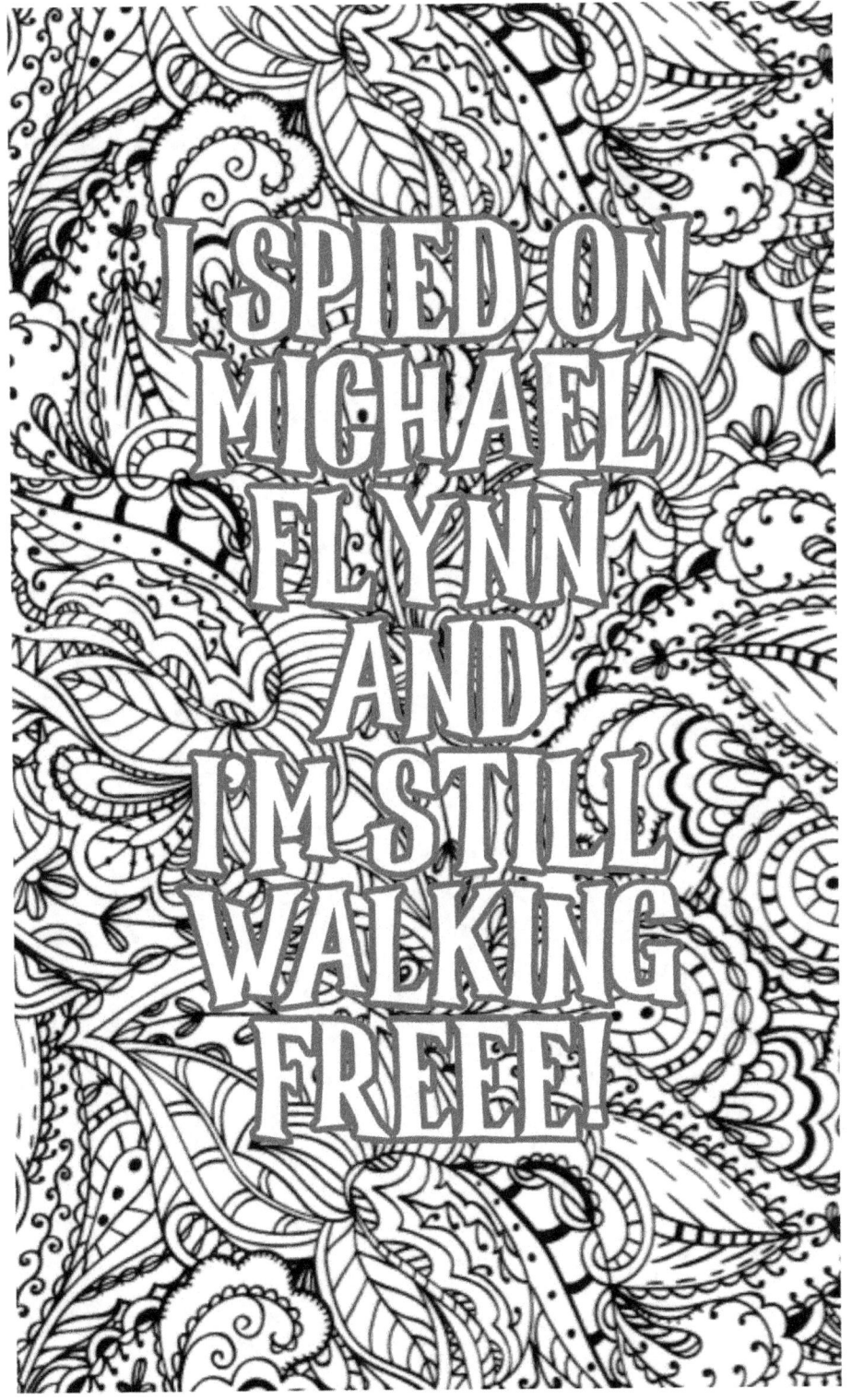

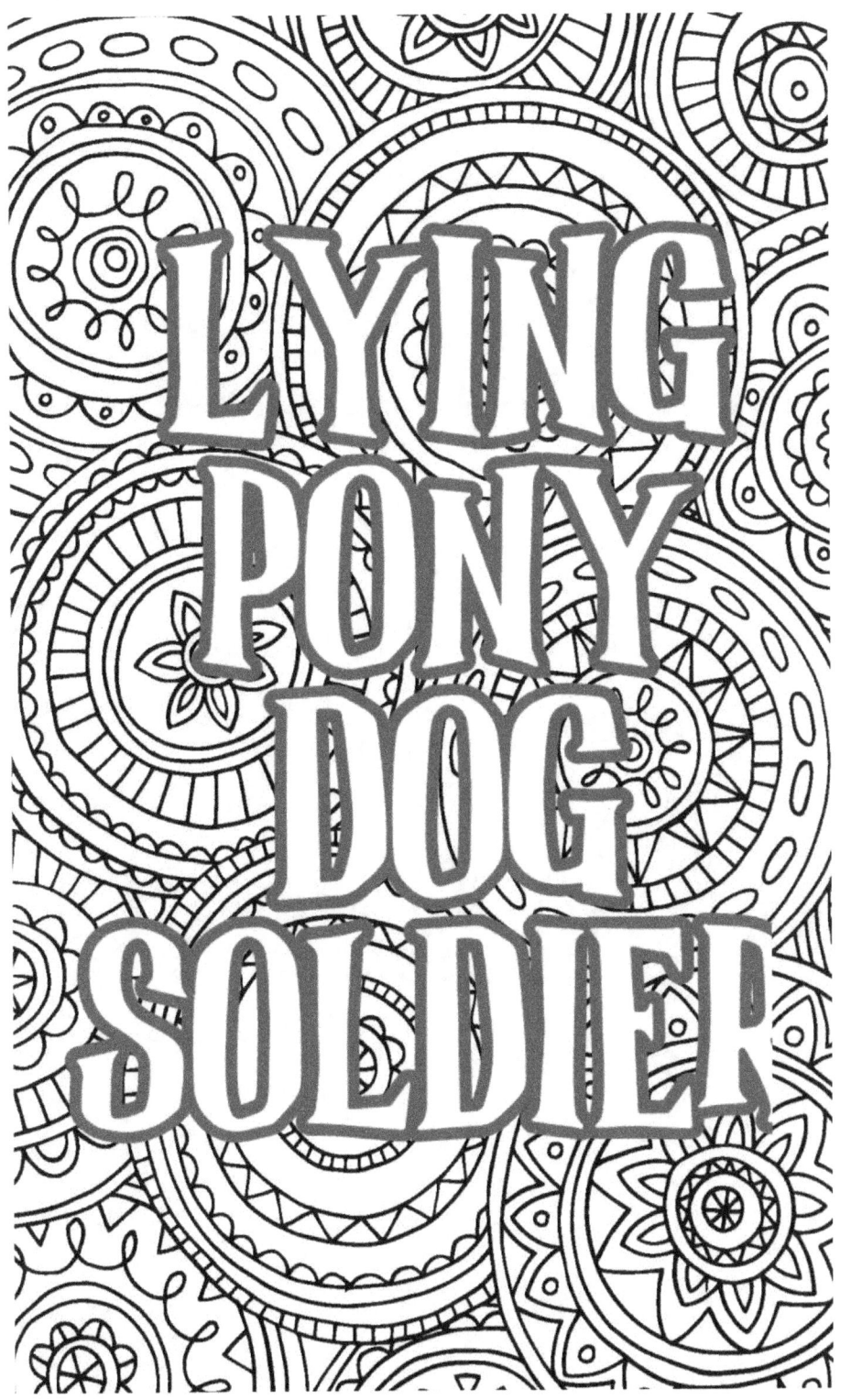

I'M RUSHING IN MY HEAD AIN'T I?

YOU KNOW THE THING

POOR KIDS ARE AS TALENTED AS WHITE KIDS

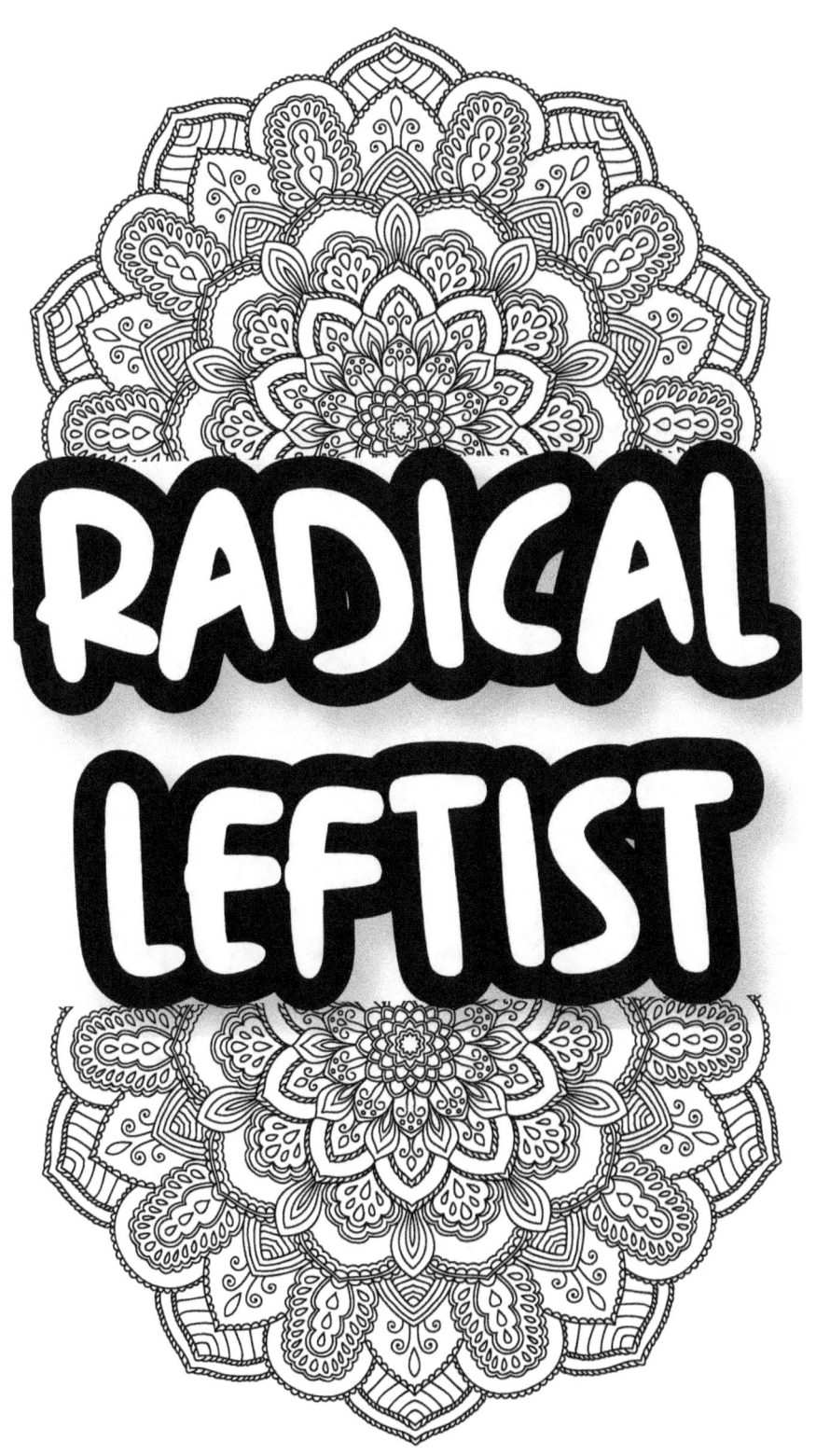

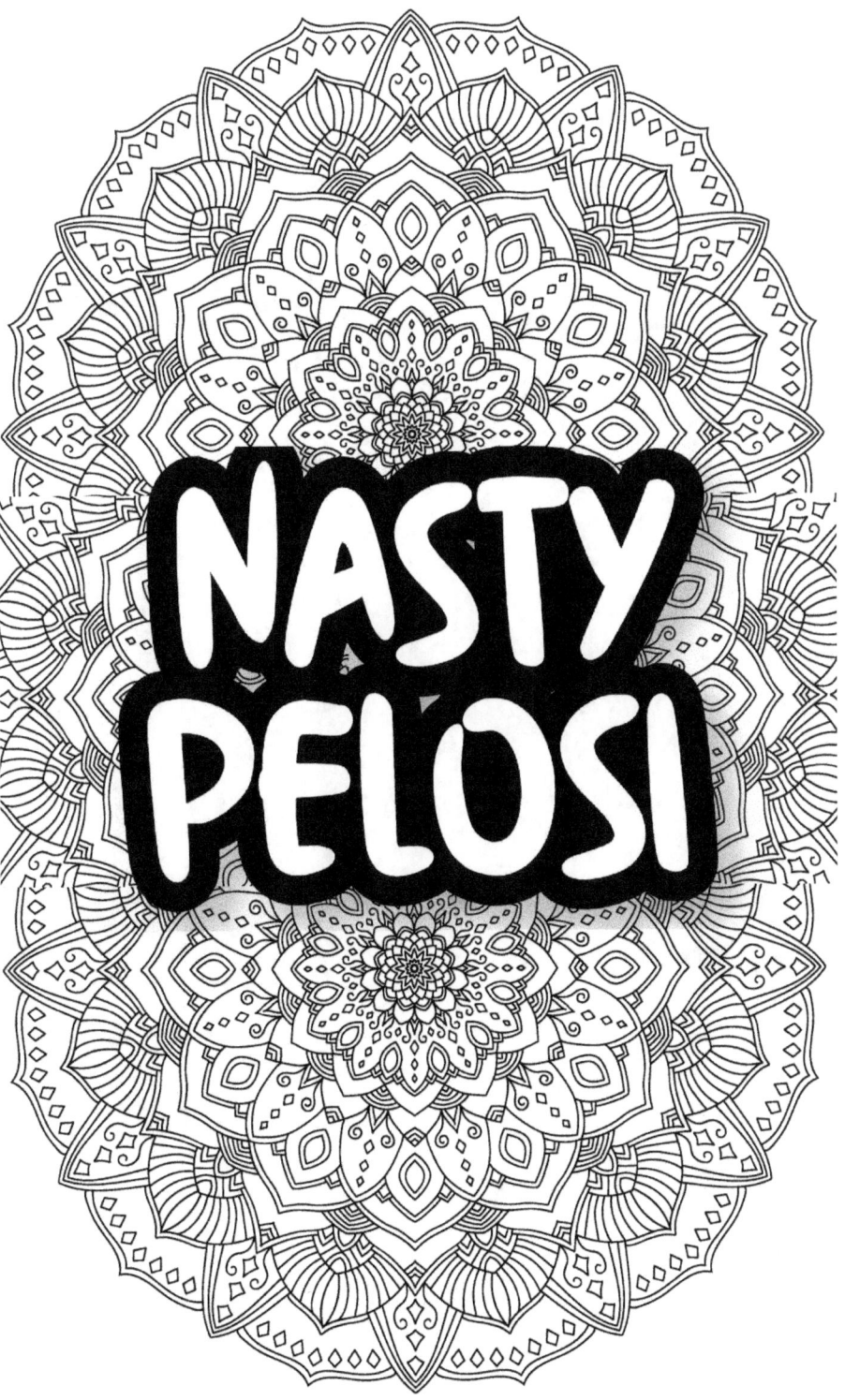

I DON'T WORK FOR YOU

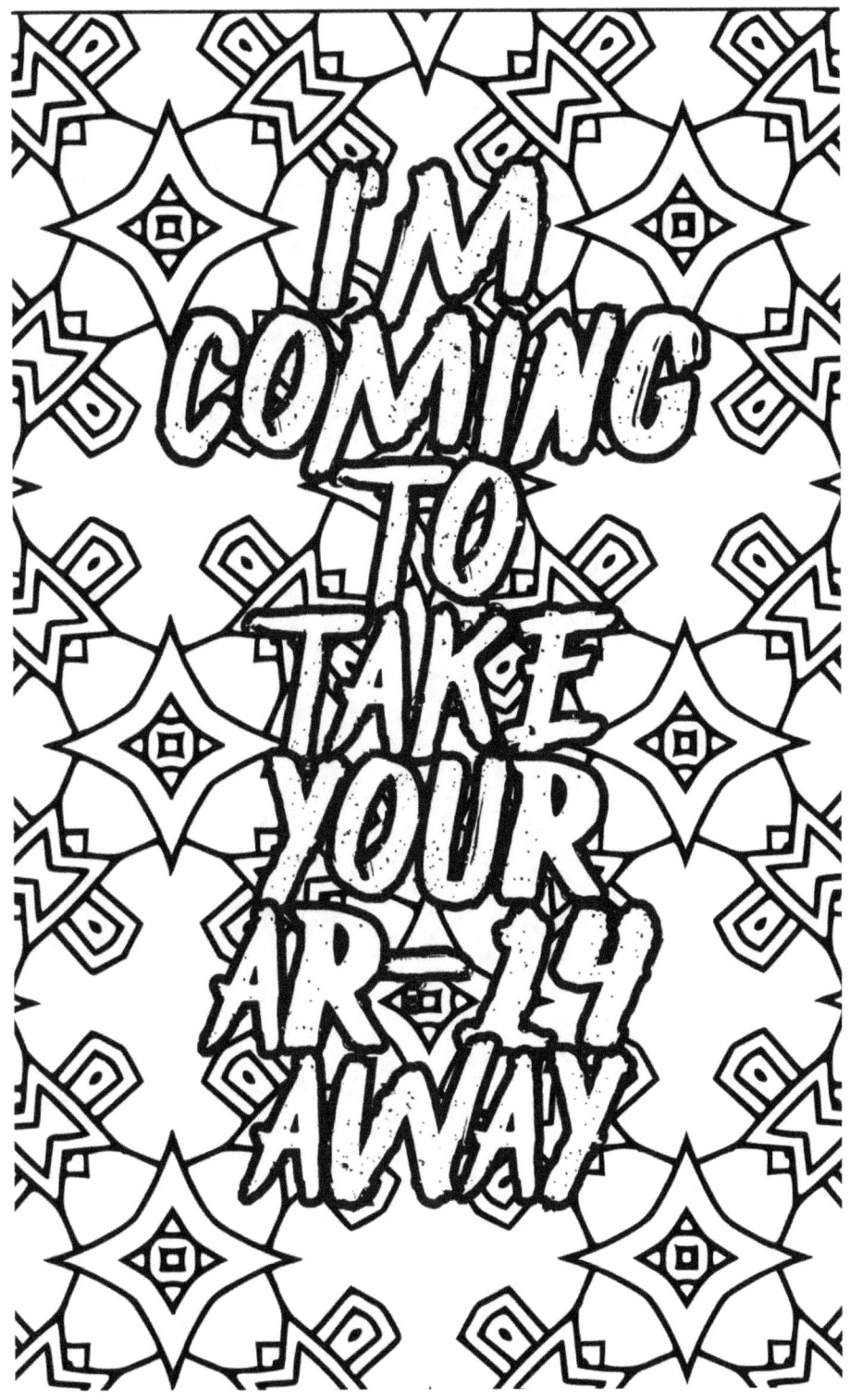

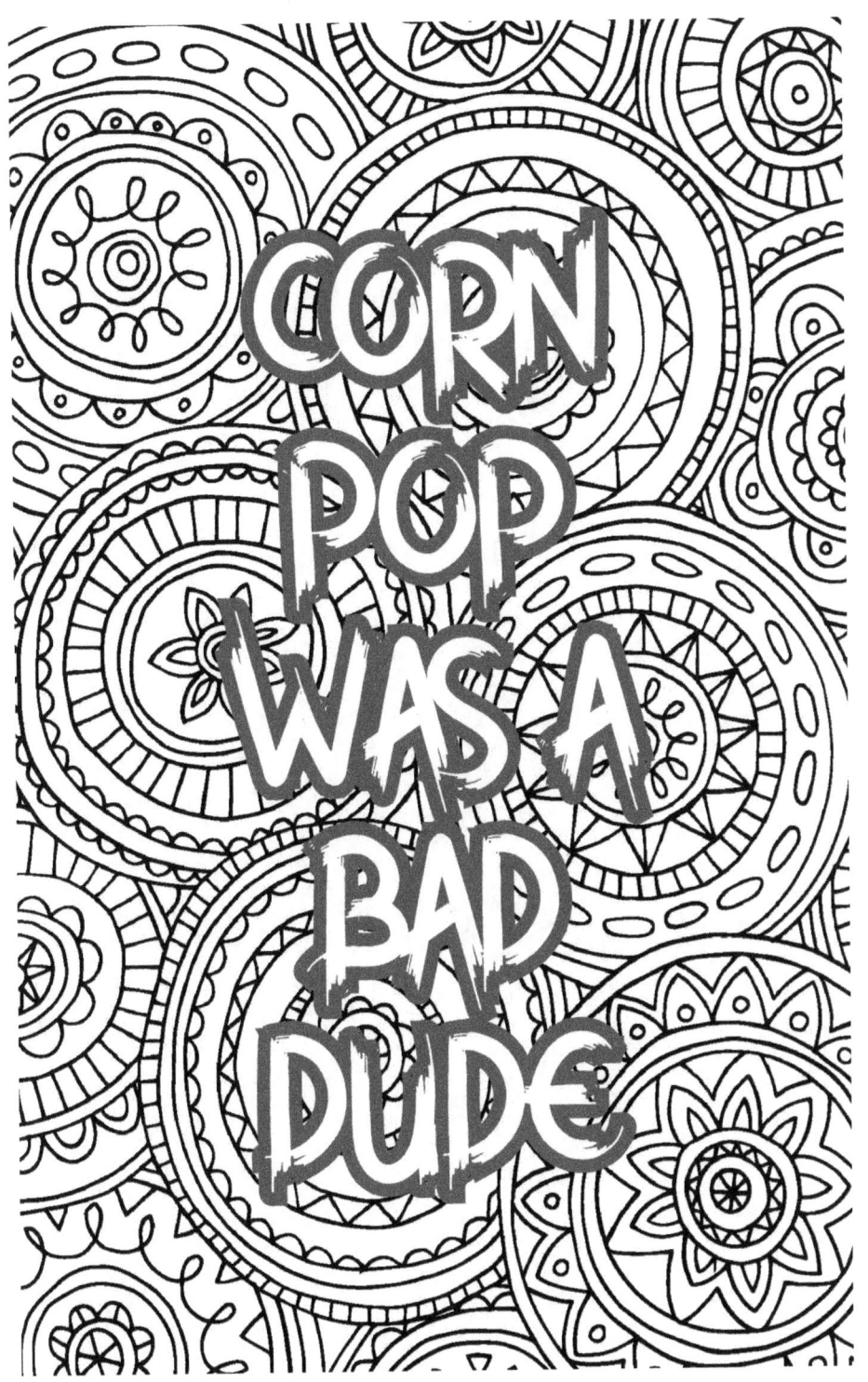

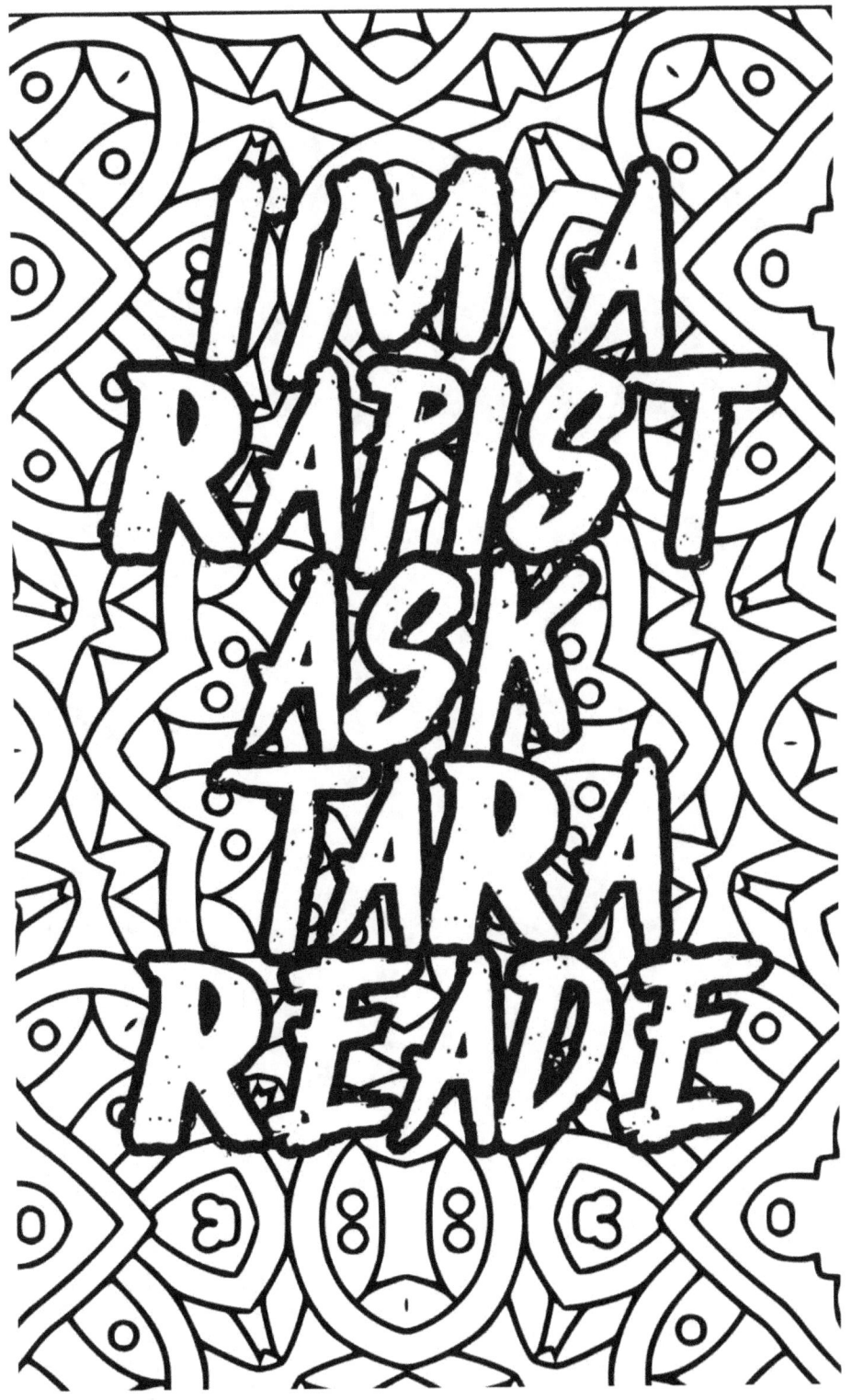

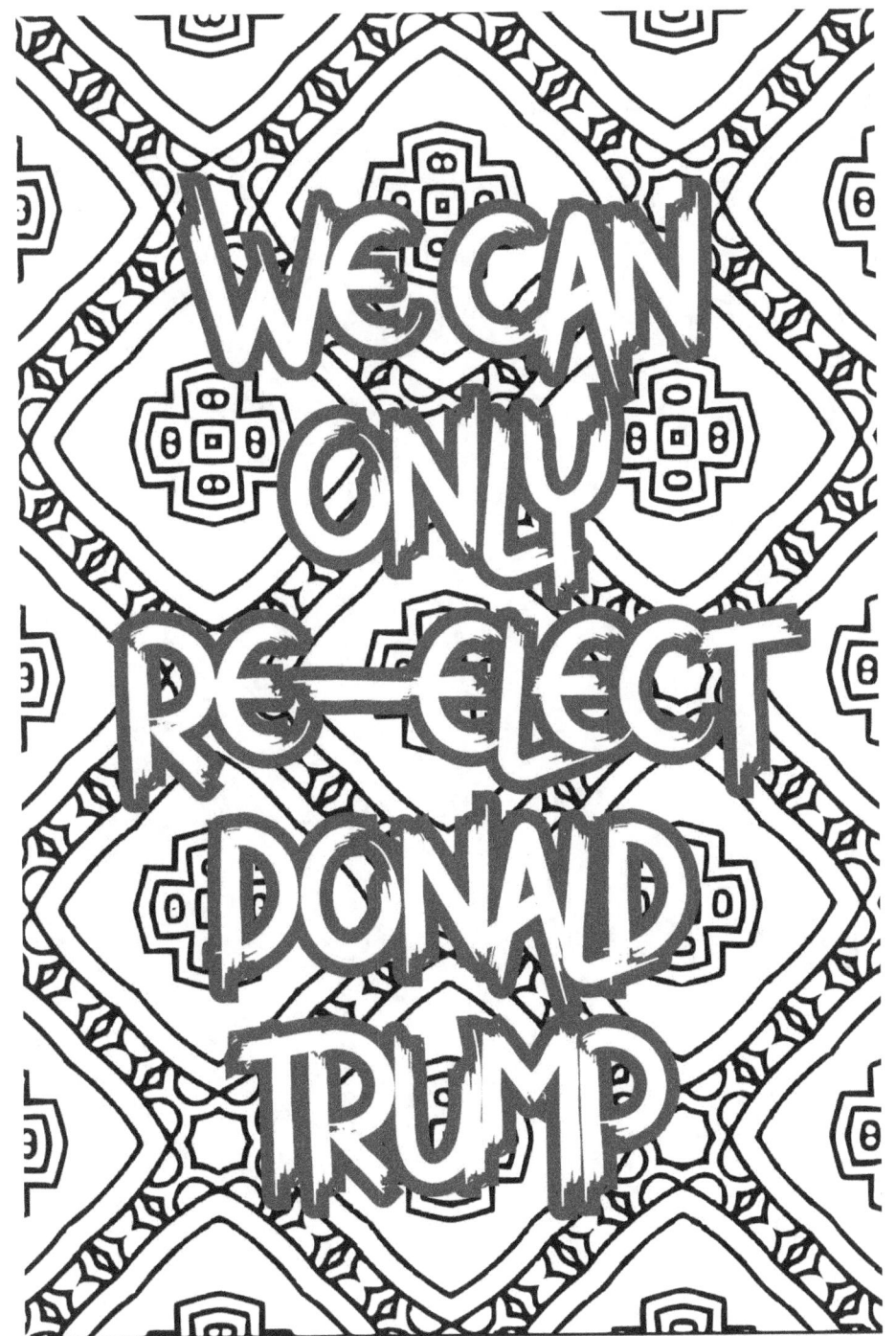

Sorry, Who the hell is Joe Biden?
—Joe Biden

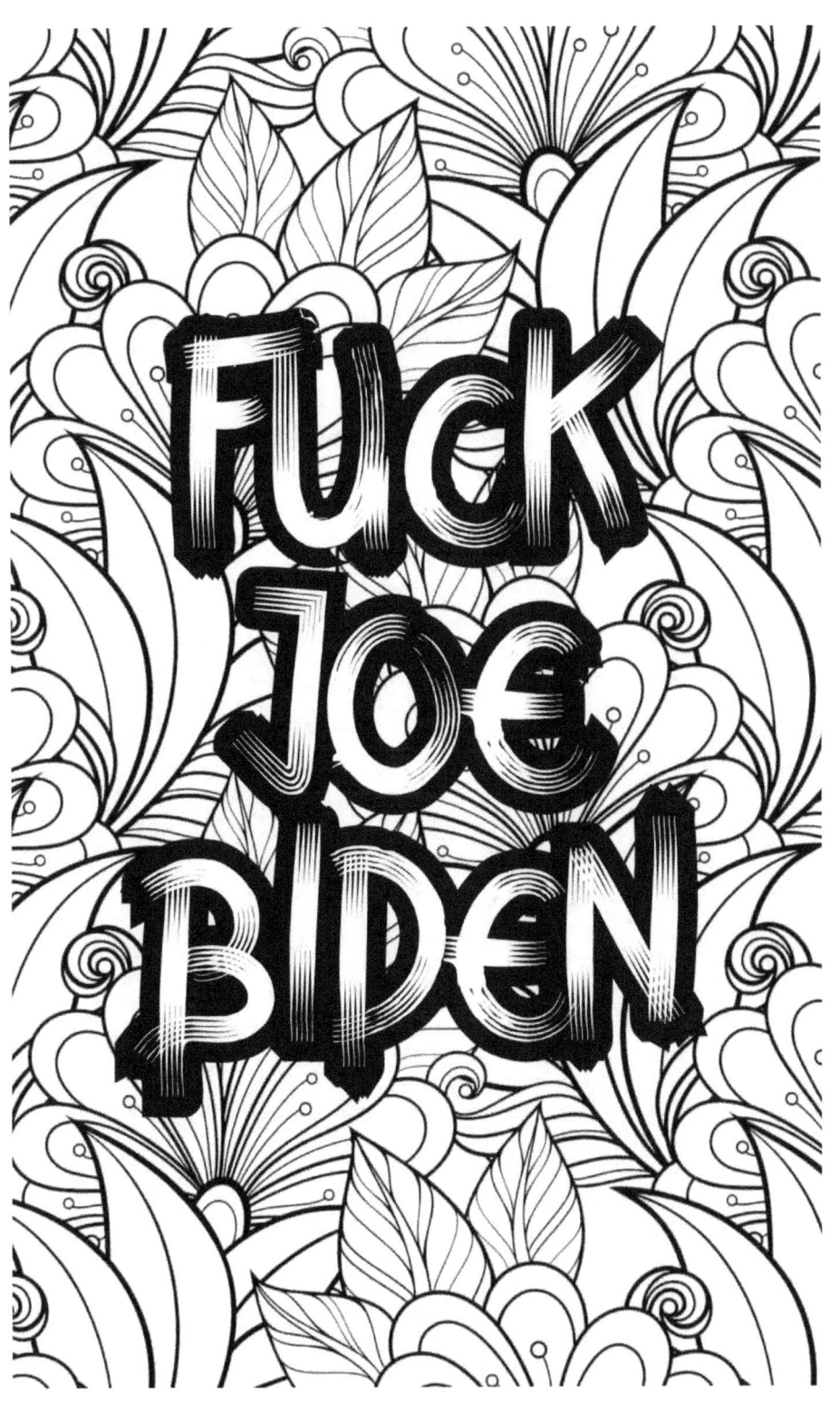

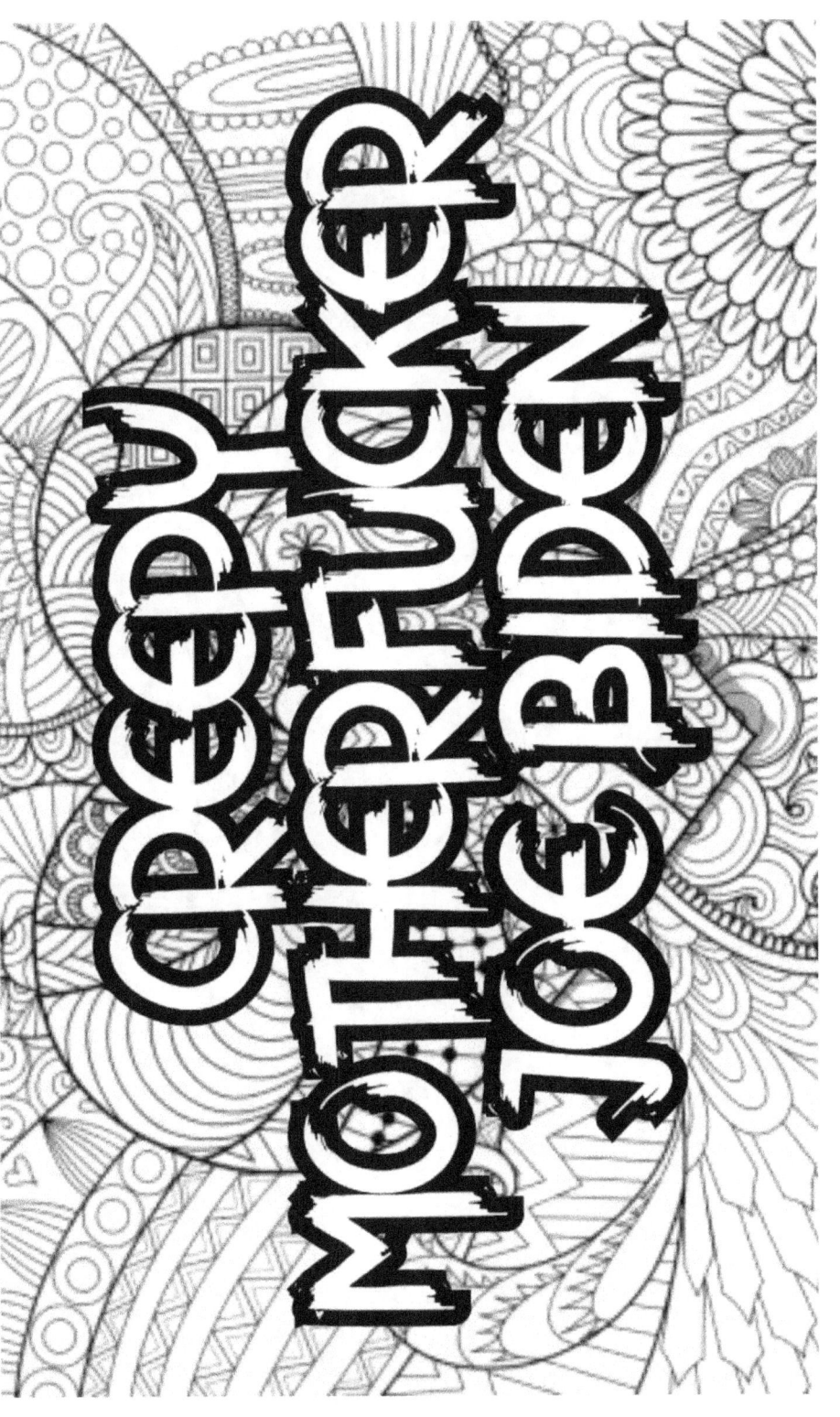

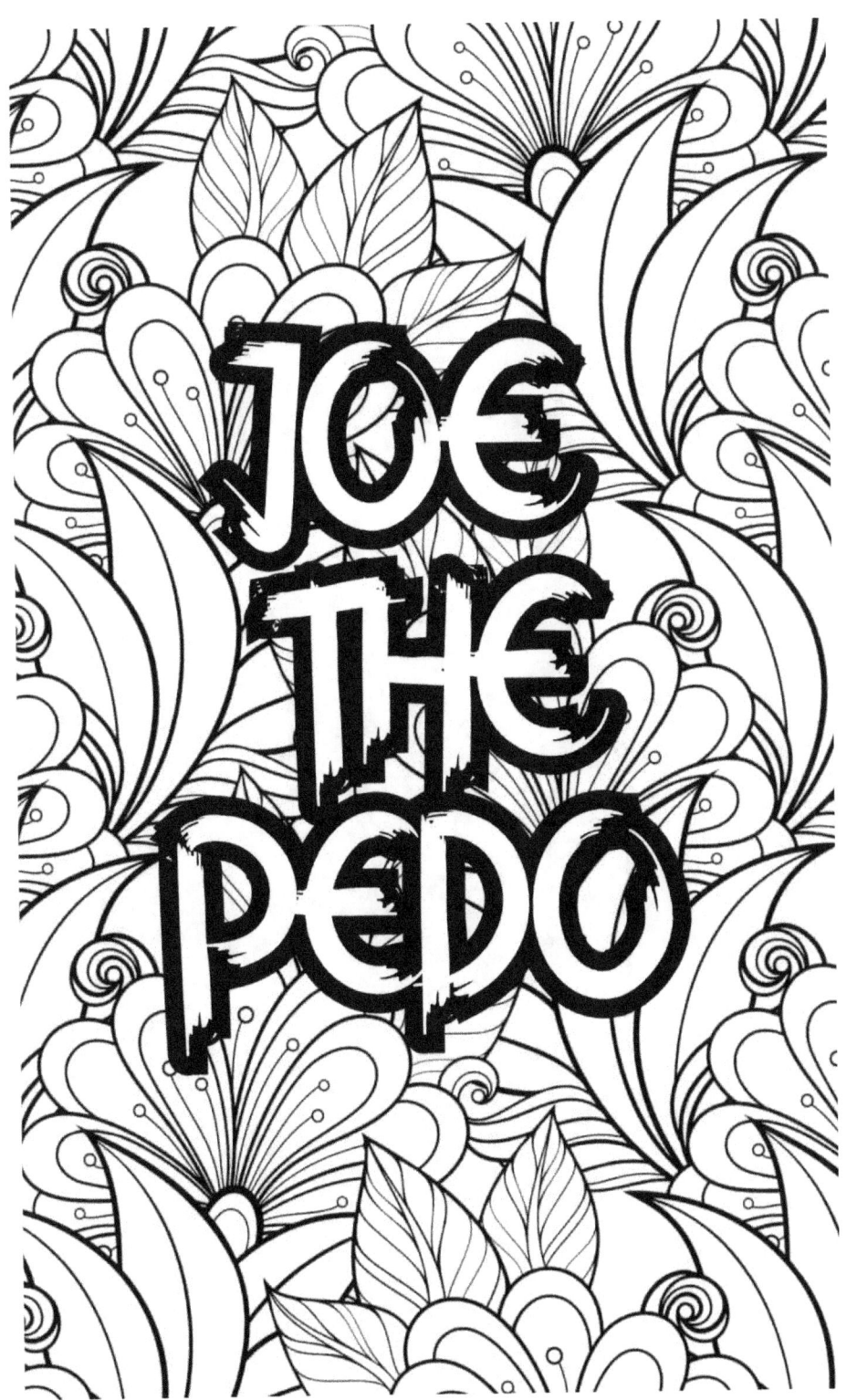

GIVE ME A BREAK!

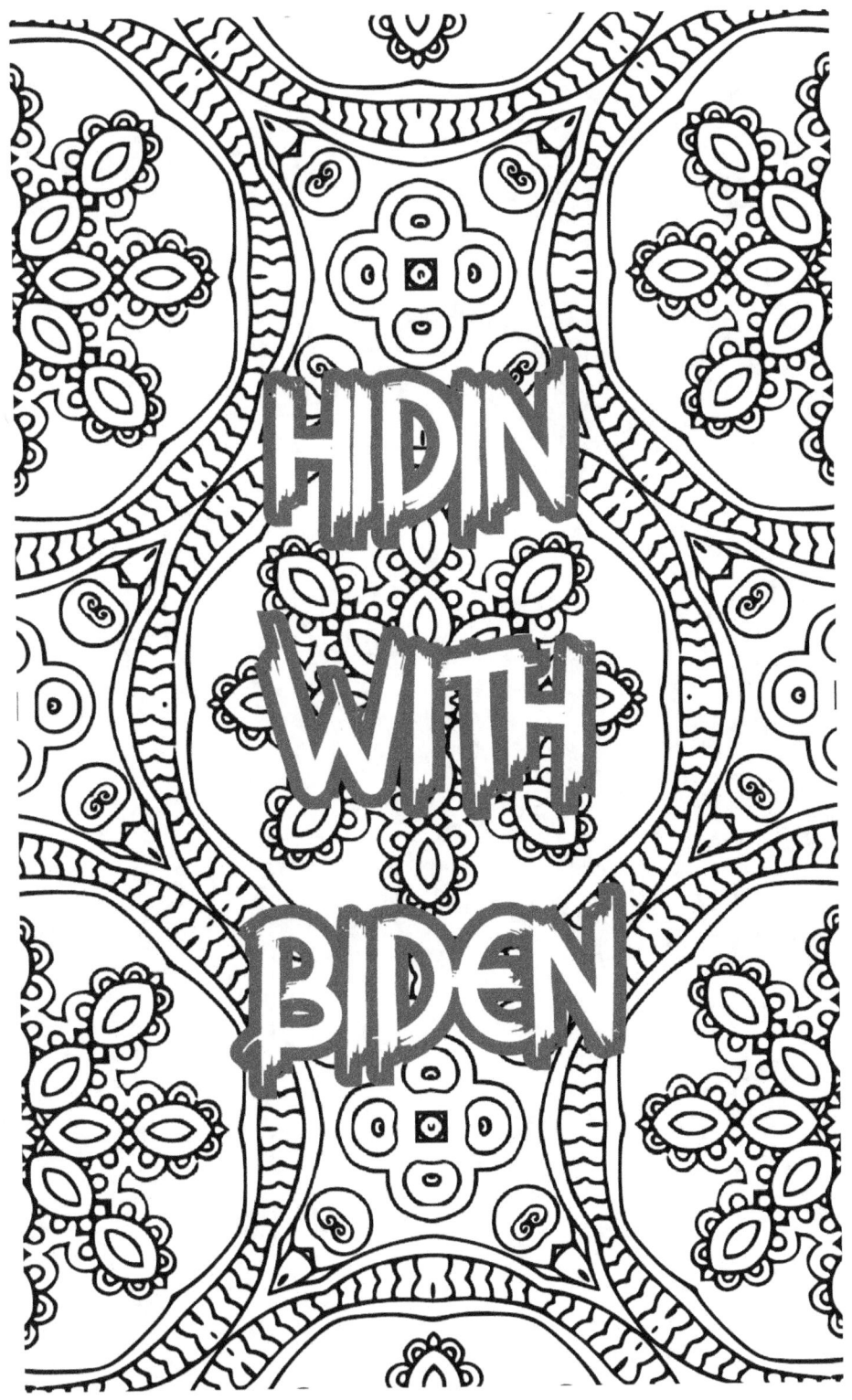

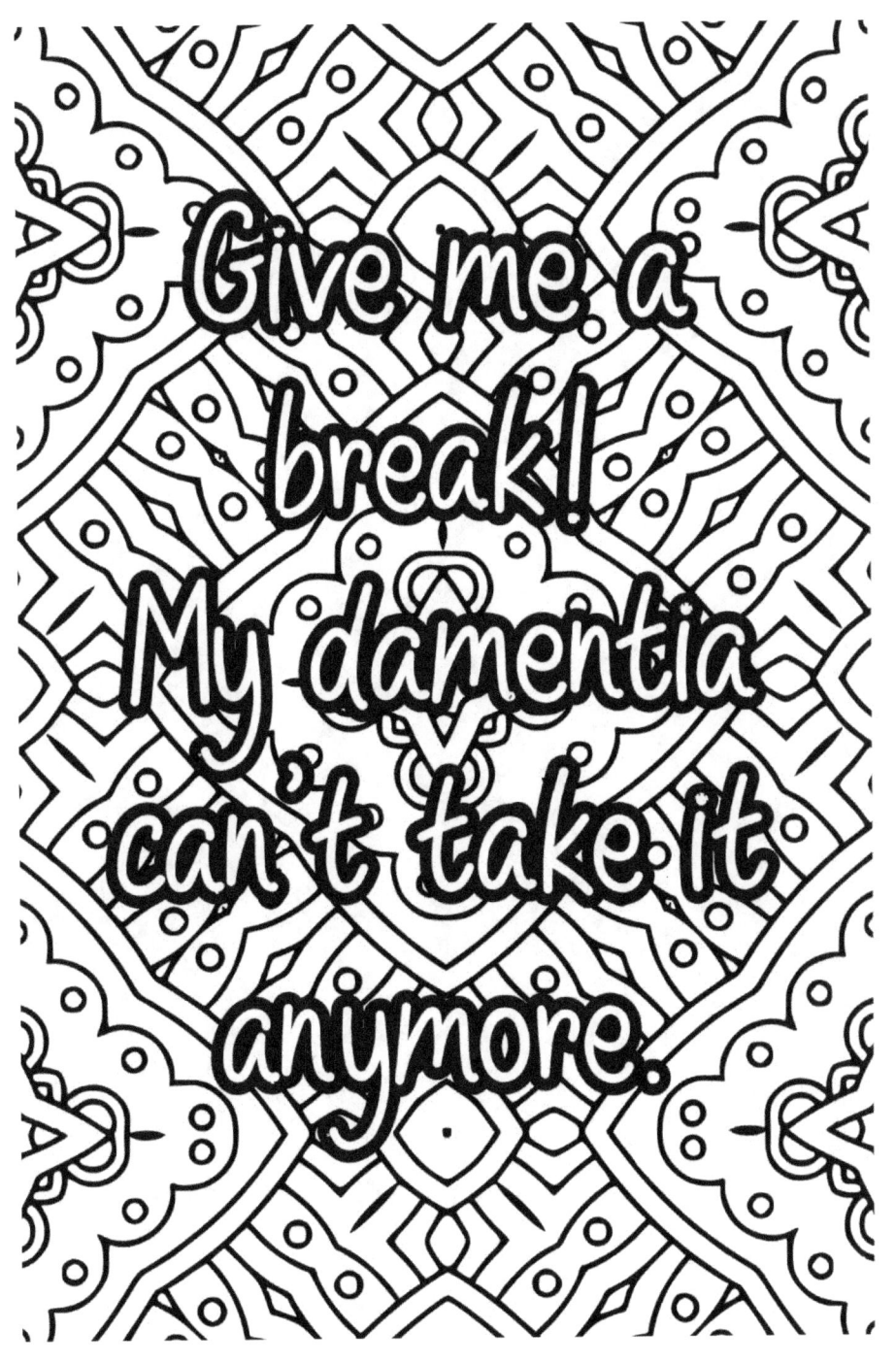

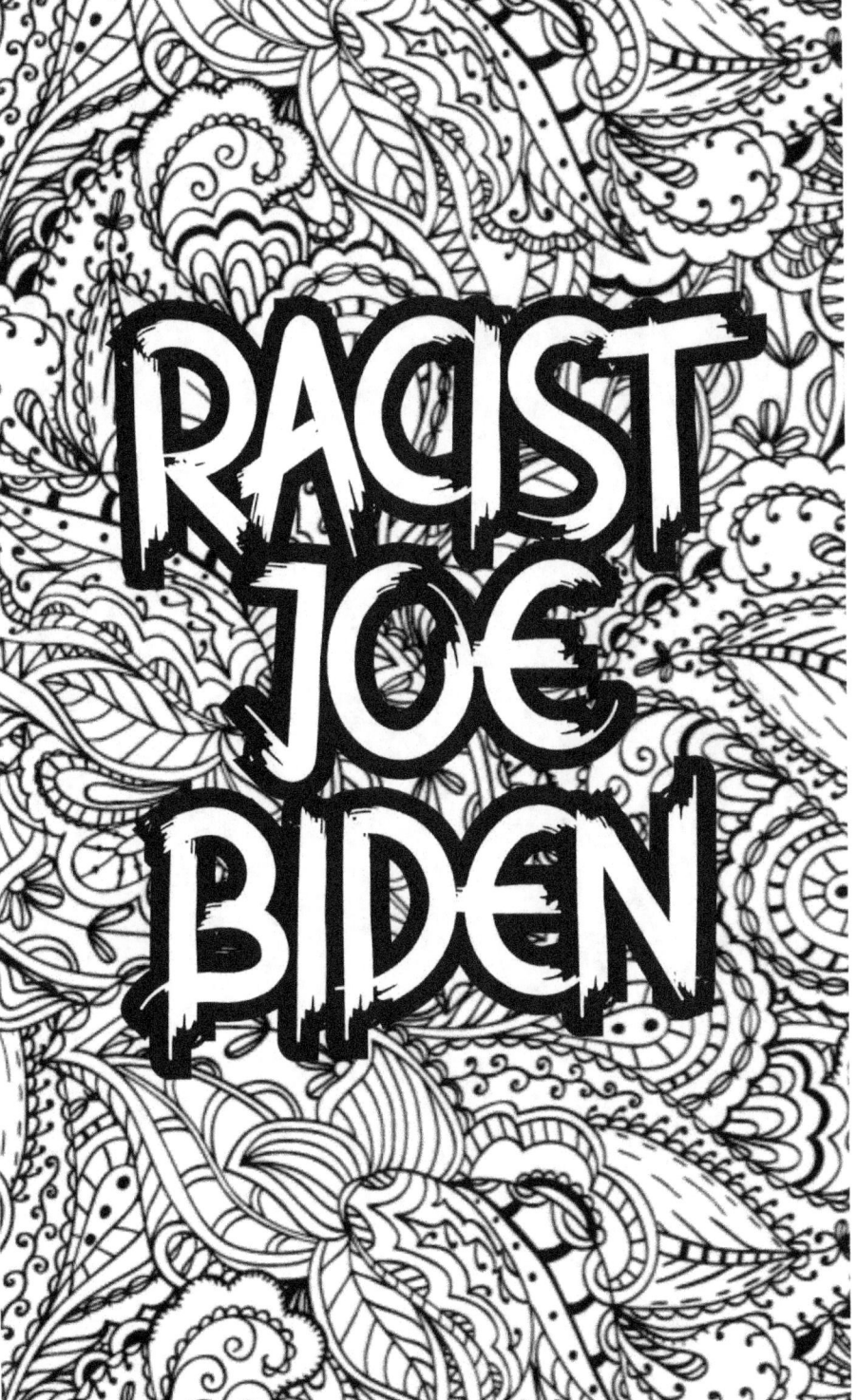

ALL
MEN AND
WOMEN
CREATED
BY
YOU KNOW
THE THING

MY LONG FRIEND TIME FRIEND SHE'S BEEN A FRIEND OF MINE

PLAY THE RADIO MAKE SURE YOU HAVE THE RECORD PLAYER IS ON

ALL
WOMEN
ARE
TO BE
BELIEVED
EXCEPT
TARA READE

YOU ARE A WHORES ASS

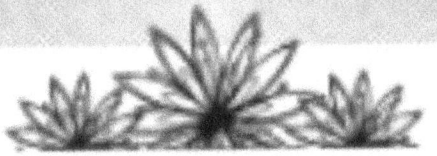

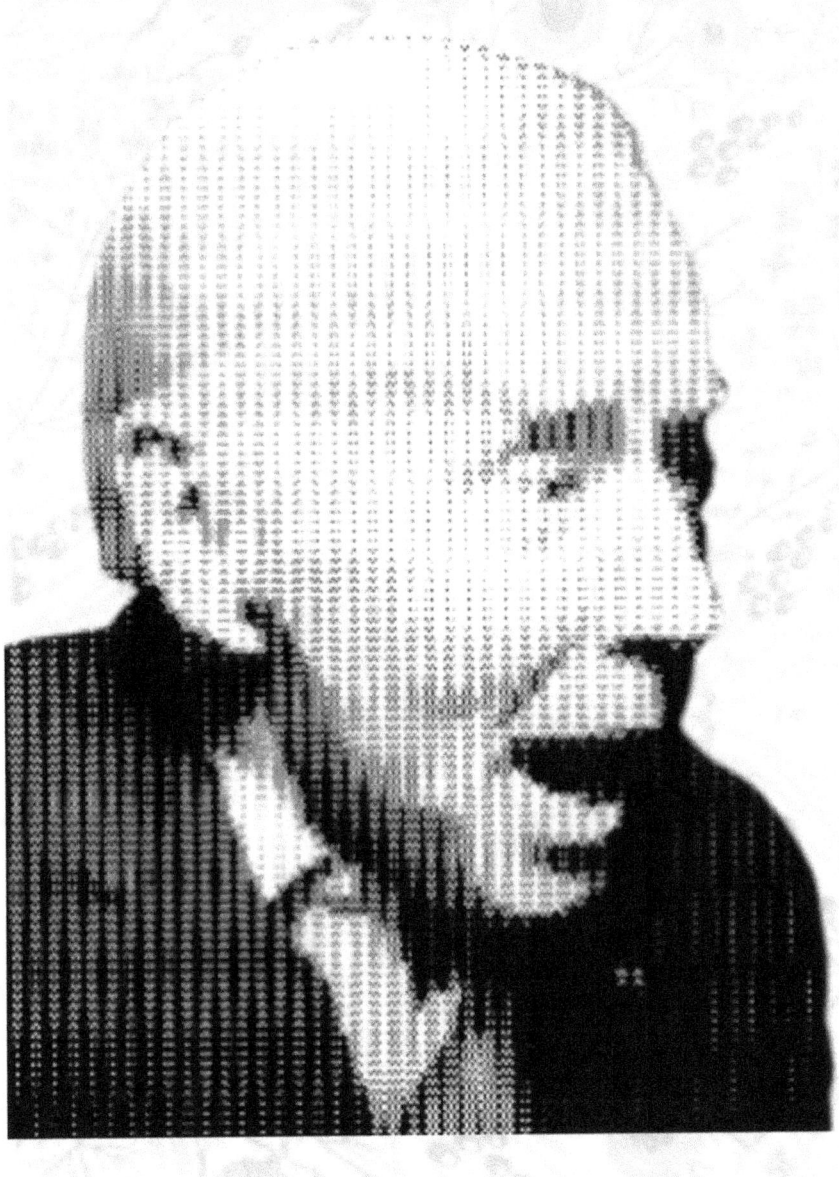

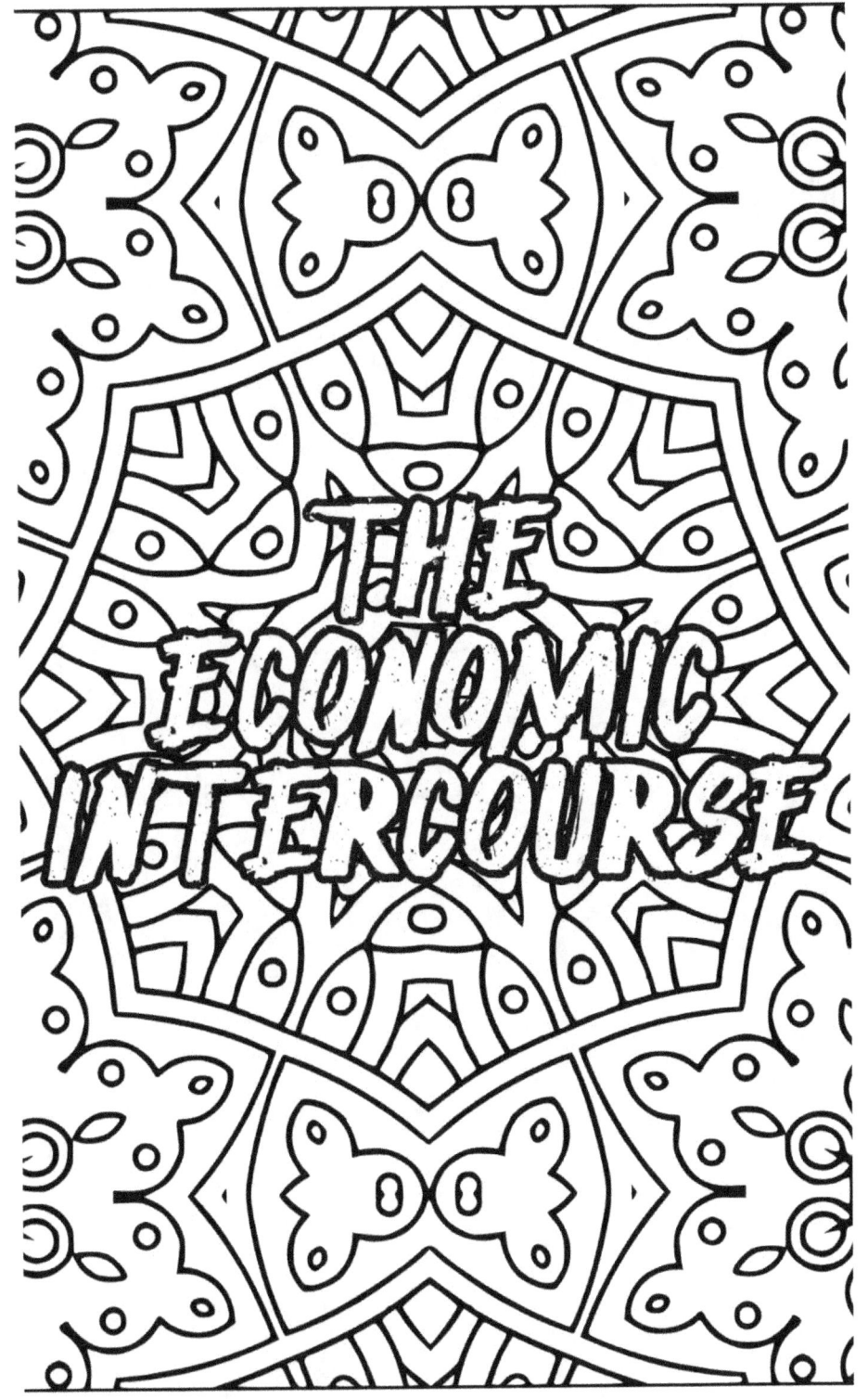

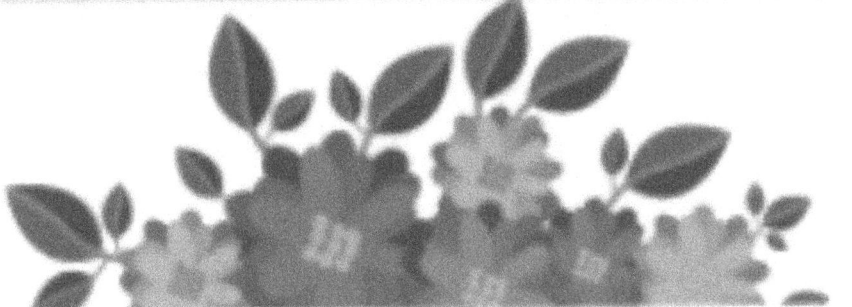

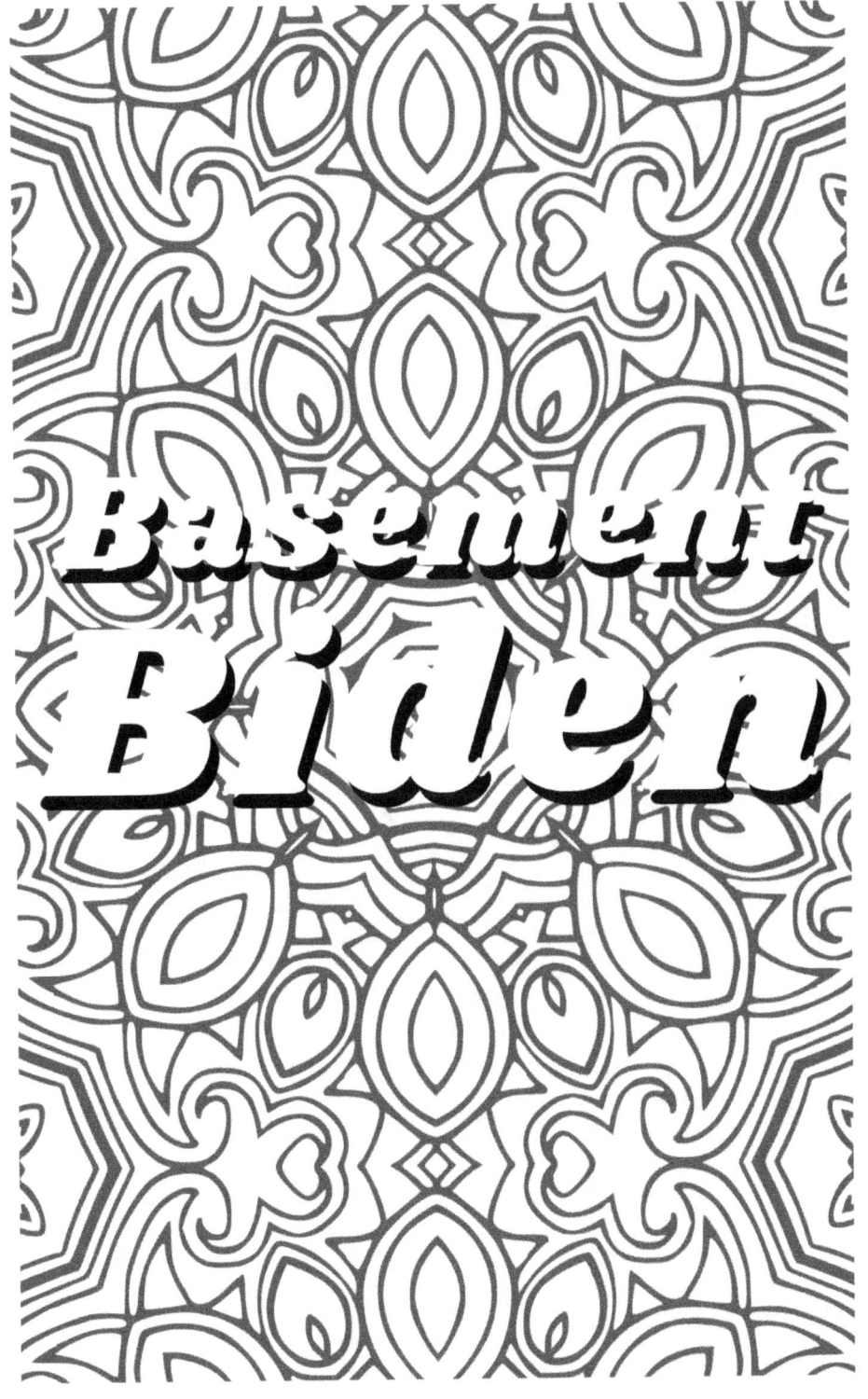

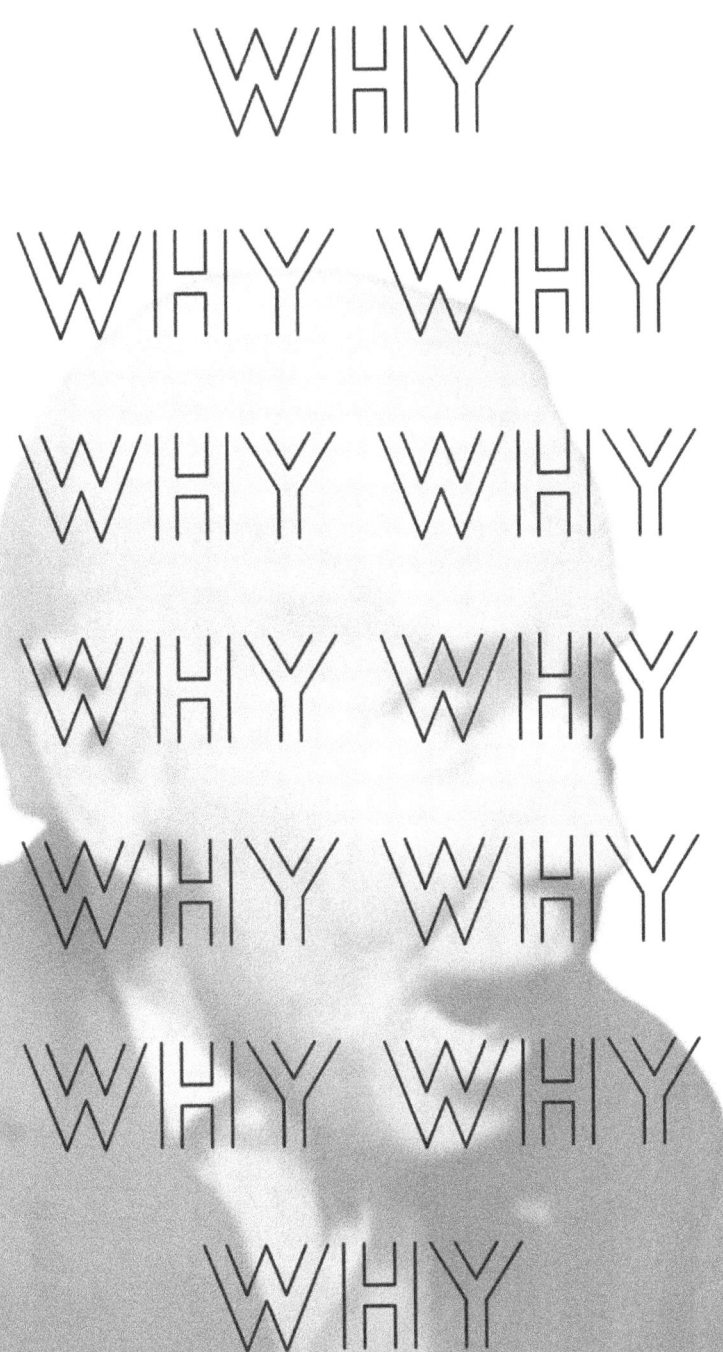

4 TRILLION OUT OF 2 BILLION

TRUMP 2020

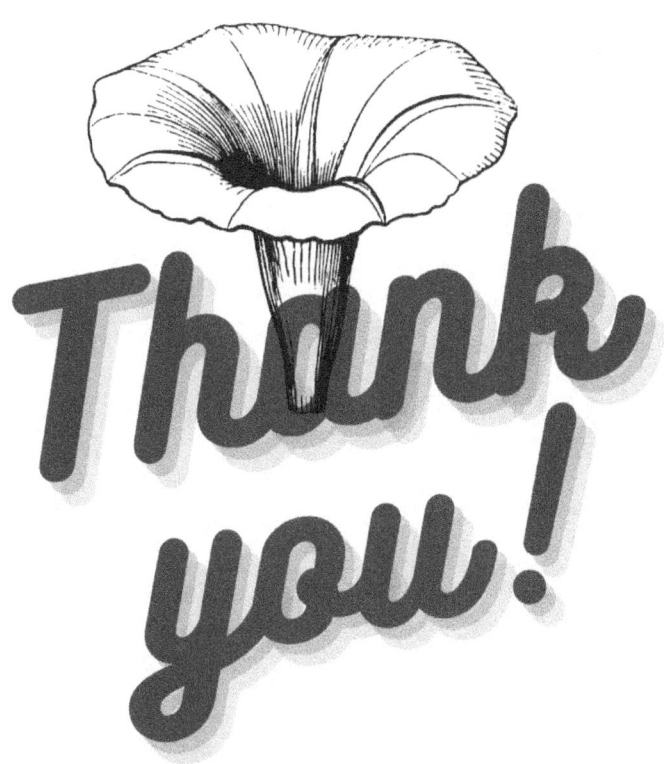

Thank you!

www.ingramcontent.com/pod-product-compliance
Lightning Source LLC
Chambersburg PA
CBHW050252220526
45465CB00002B/655